DOT MARKERS
NEW TESTAMENT
ACTIVITY BOOK FOR KIDS

BIG DOTS

Single-sided pages – Ages 2+

THIS BOOK BELONGS TO:

_____

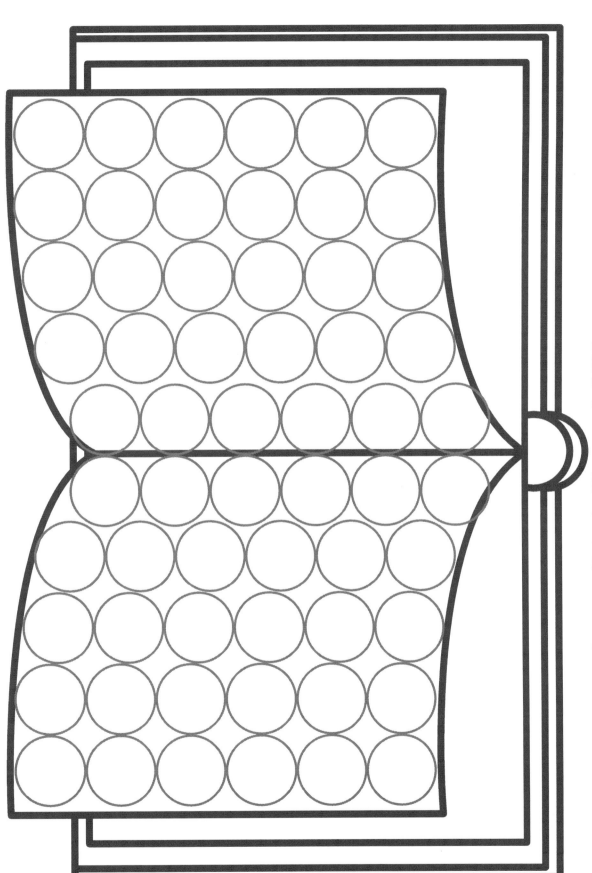

I LOVE TO READ THE SCRIPTURES

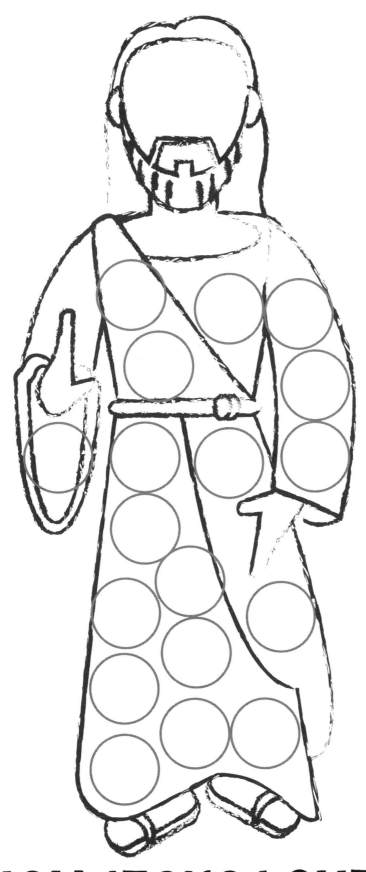

I KNOW JESUS LOVES ME

AN ANGEL TOLD MARY &

JOSEPH THAT JESUS WOULD BE BORN

ZACHARIAS & ELISABETH'S PRAYERS
WERE ANSWERED & THEY HAD A BABY
NAMED JOHN

MARY & JOSEPH TRAVELED TO
BETHLEHEM

MARY & JOSEPH COULDN'T FIND ROOM TO STAY AT ANY OF THE INNS

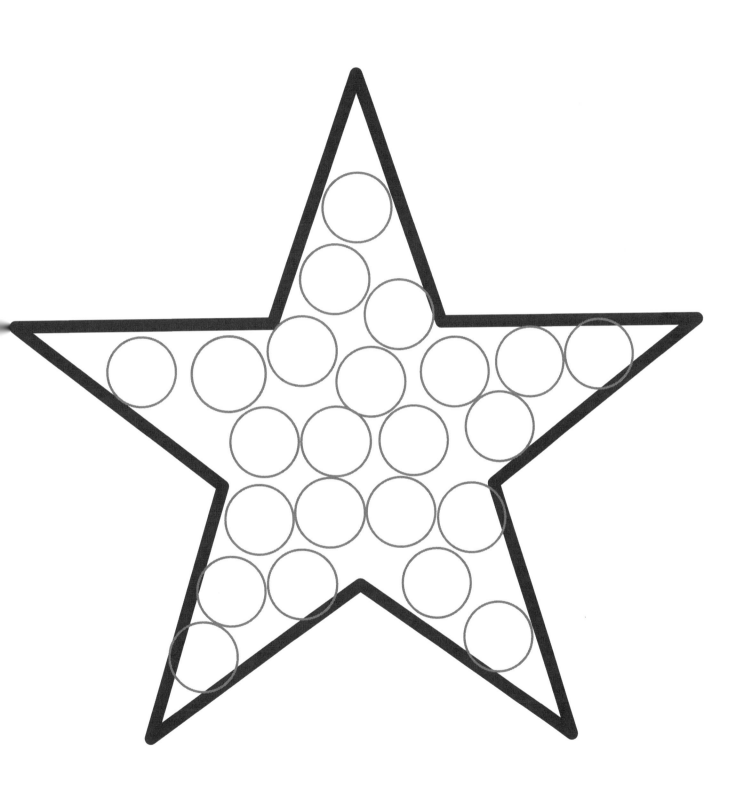

A BRIGHT STAR APPEARED IN THE SKY
TO SIGNAL THE SAVIOR'S BIRTH

JESUS WAS BORN IN BETHLEHEM

JESUS WAS BORN IN A MANGER
SURROUNDED BY ANIMALS

SHEPHERDS CAME TO SEE BABY JESUS

THE WISE MEN TRAVELED TO BRING GIFTS TO JESUS

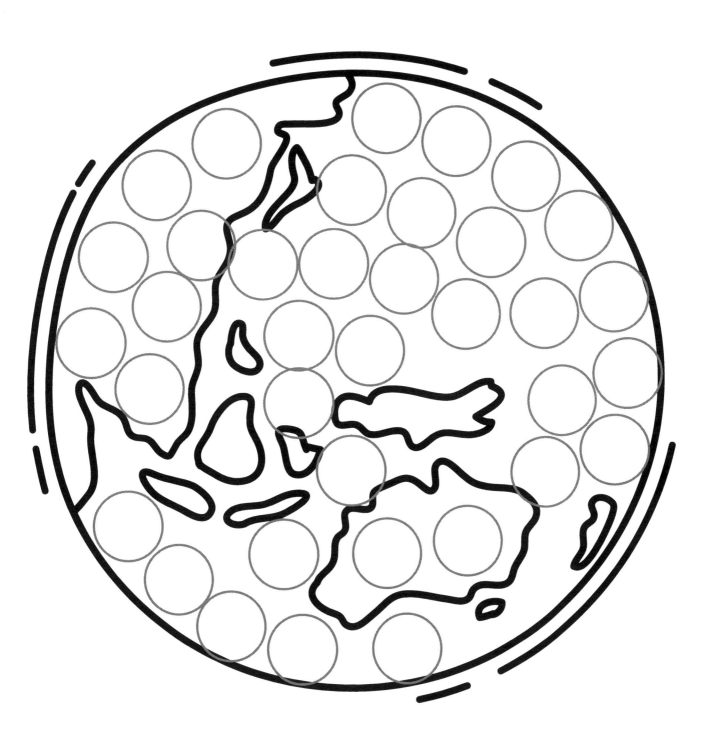

JESUS CREATED EVERYTHING
ON THE EARTH

JESUS CHRIST IS OUR LIGHT

JESUS CHRIST WAS BAPTIZED

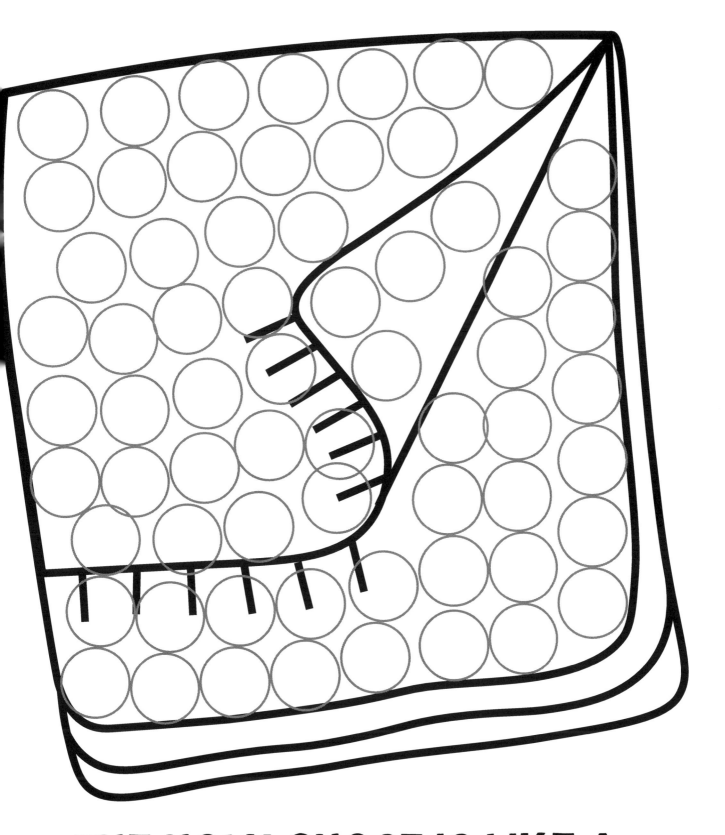

THE HOLY GHOST IS LIKE A BLANKET & COMFORTS US

JESUS WANTS US TO BE
FISHERS OF MEN

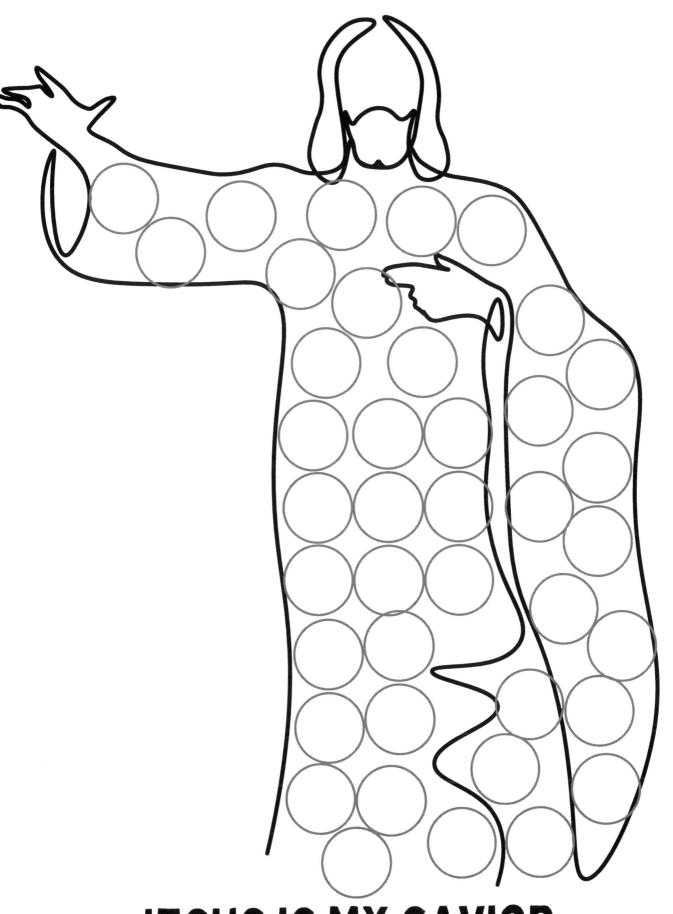

JESUS IS MY SAVIOR

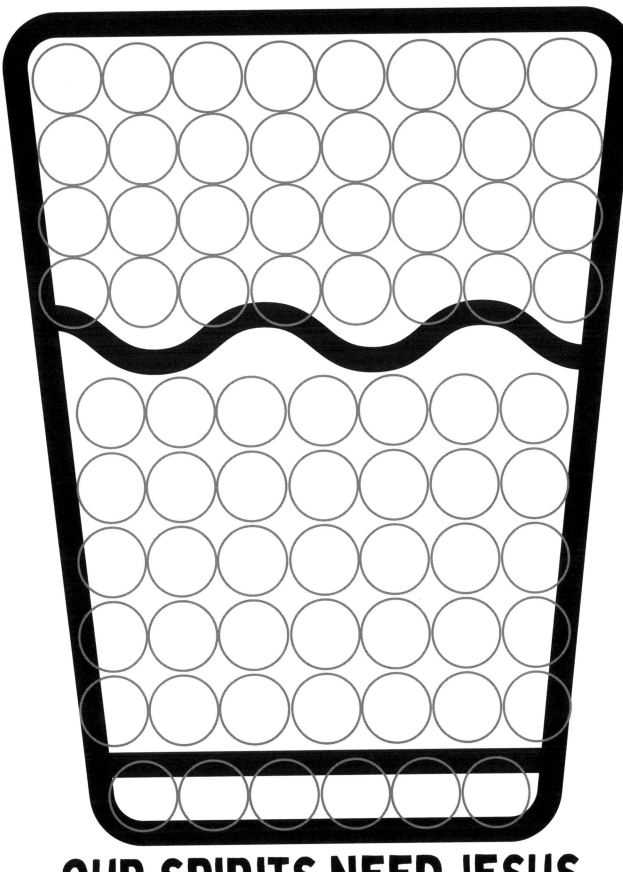

OUR SPIRITS NEED JESUS

CHRIST`S LIVING WATER

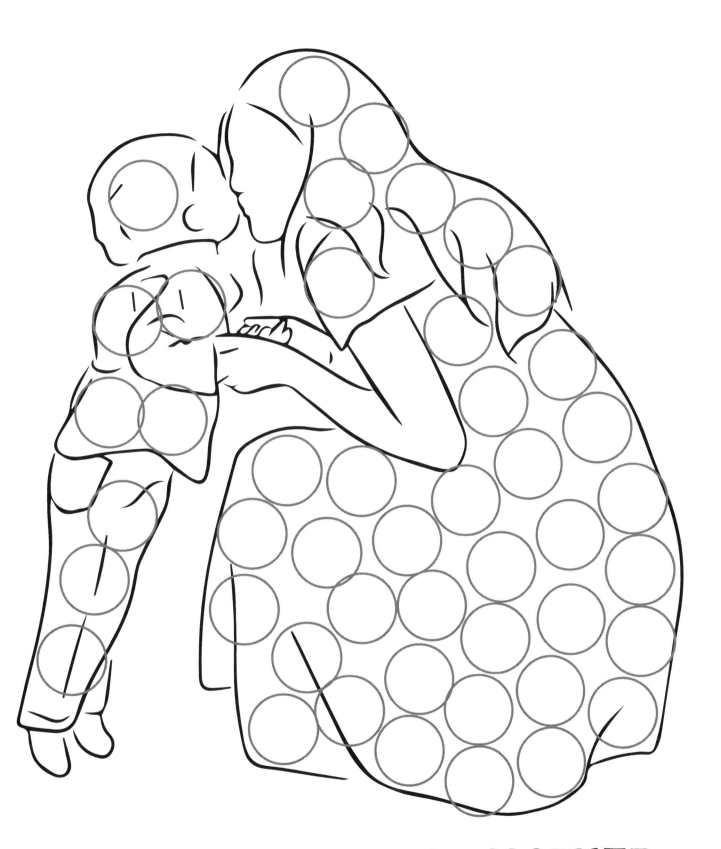

JESUS HONORED HIS MOTHER

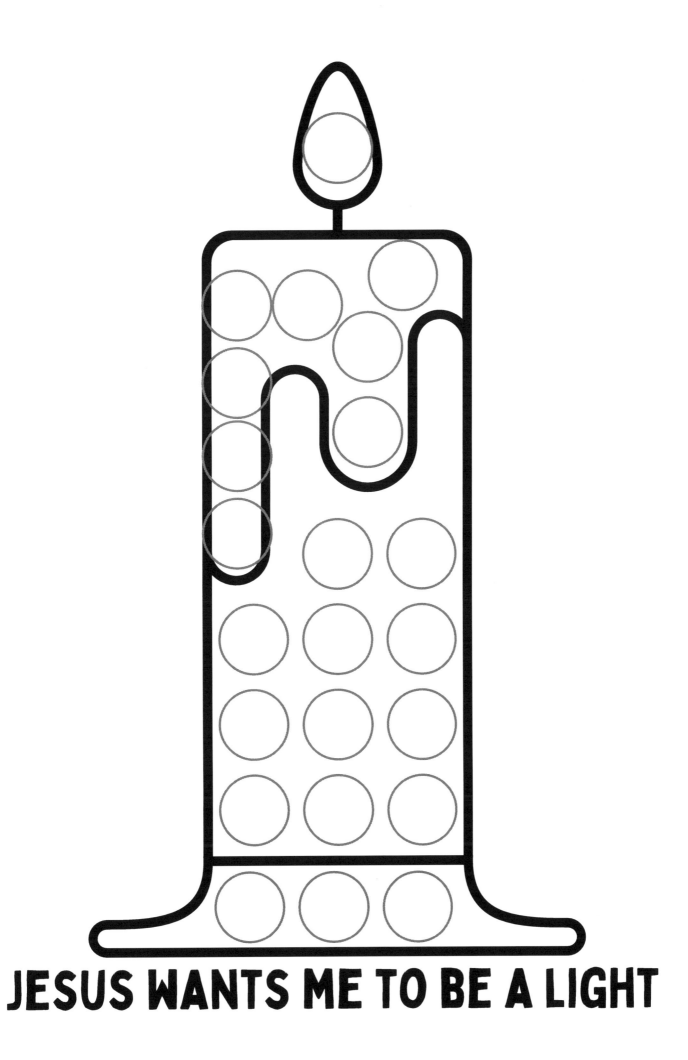

JESUS WANTS ME TO BE A LIGHT

JESUS WANTS ME TO LOVE EVERYONE

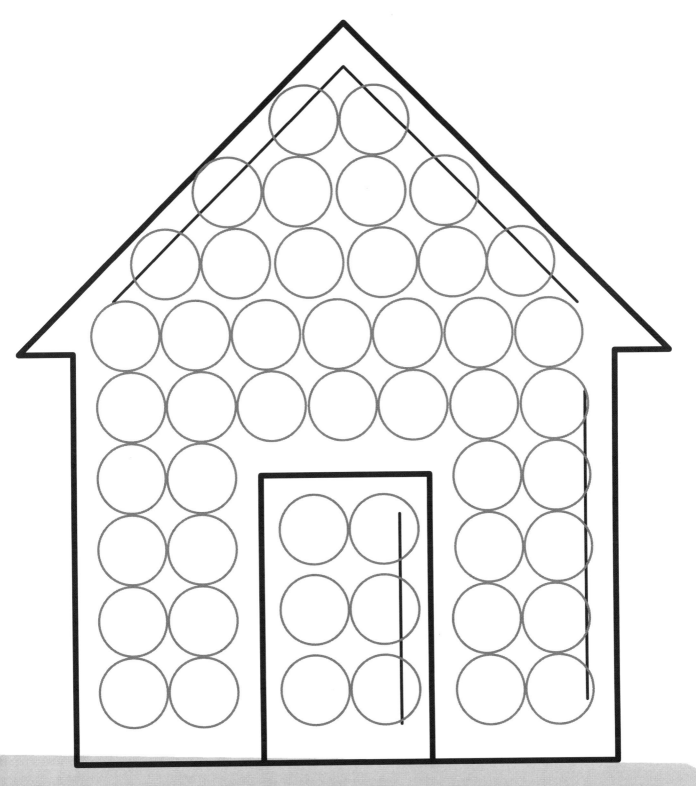

THE WISE MAN BUILT HIS HOUSE
UPON A ROCK

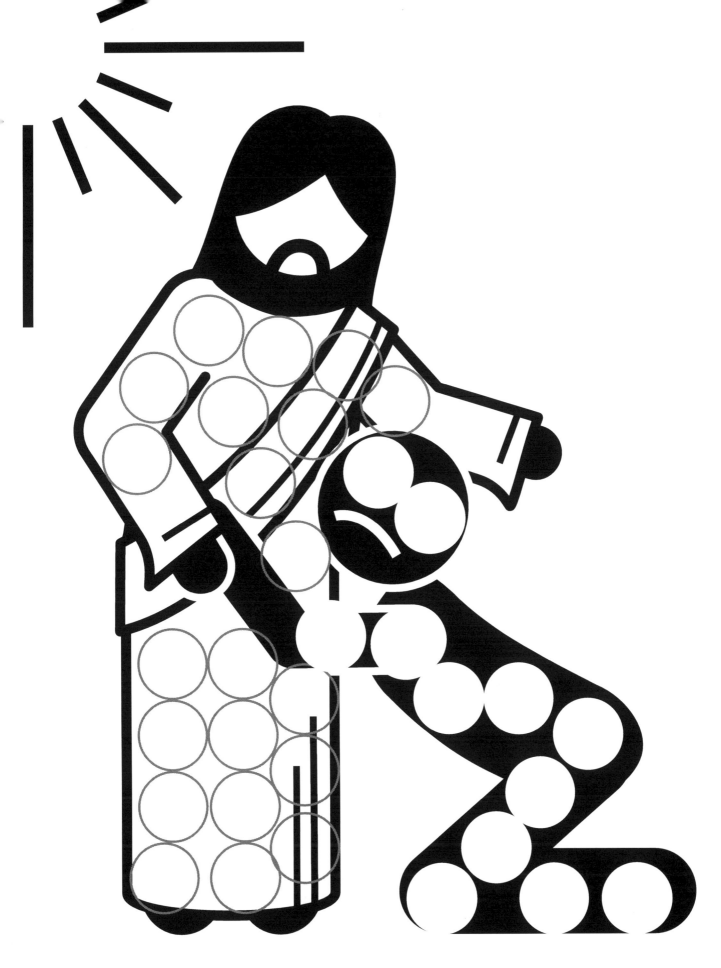

JESUS PERFORMED MANY MIRACLES

I CAN SERVE OTHERS

JESUS CAN HEAL ME

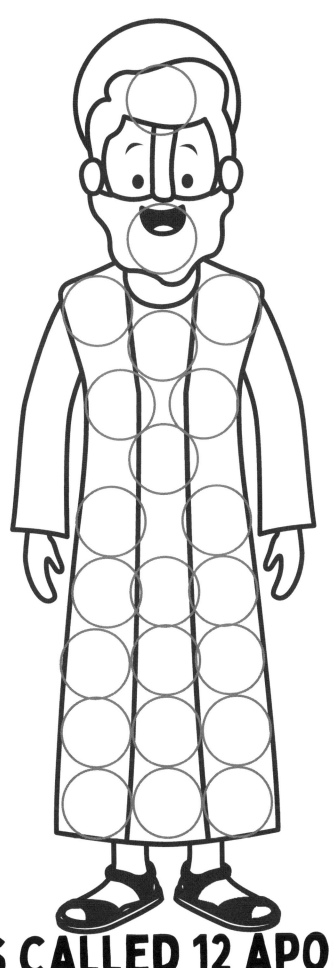

JESUS CALLED 12 APOSTLES

I CAN KEEP THE SABBATH DAY HOLY

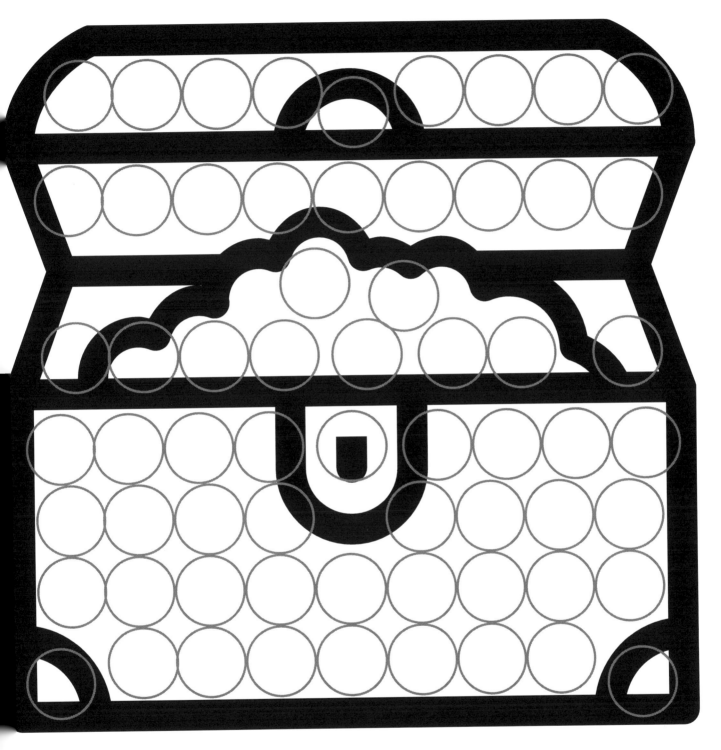

BEING A MEMBER OF CHRIST'S CHURCH IS A TREASURE

TESTIMONIES ARE LIKE SEEDS

JESUS FED 5,000 WITH 5 LOAVES & 2 FISHES

JESUS WALKED ON WATER

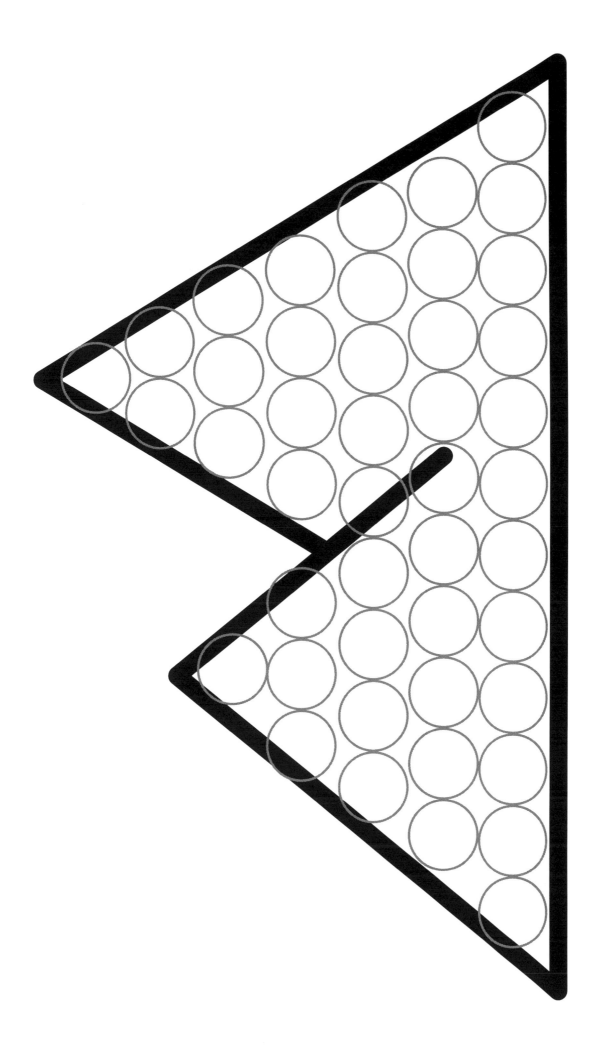

FAITH CAN MOVE MOUNTAINS

WE HAVE PRIESTHOOD KEYS ON THE EARTH TODAY

I CAN HELP OTHERS

I CAN FORGIVE OTHERS

JESUS IS THE GOOD SHEPHERD

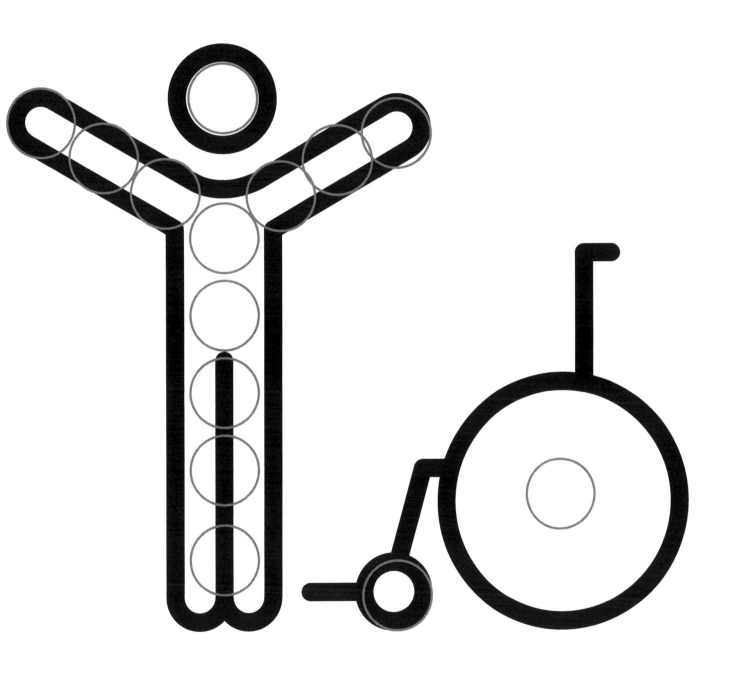

JESUS HEALED MANY

JESUS BLESSED THE CHILDREN

KEEPING THE COMMANDMENTS

HELPS ME KNOW THEY ARE TRUE

JESUS TAUGHT THE PEOPLE

JESUS KNOWS EVERYONE & WANTS EVERY LOST PERSON (COIN) TO COME BACK TO HIM

JESUS WANTS TO FIND EVERY LOST SHEEP

I CAN HELP JESUS FIND
HIS LOST SHEEP

JESUS CALMED THE
STORMY SEA

JESUS TAUGHT THAT LIKE A CUP, WE NEED TO BE CLEAN ON THE OUTSIDE & INSIDE

JESUS KNOWS MY NAME

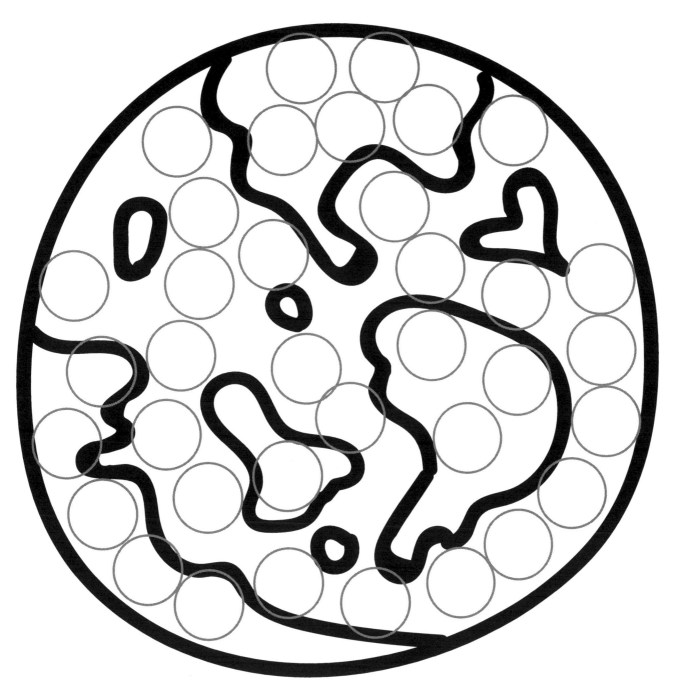

THE GOSPEL WILL BE PREACHED TO ALL THE WORLD BEFORE THE SAVIOR COMES AGAIN

I AM RESPONSIBLE FOR PUTTING OIL IN MY OWN LAMP

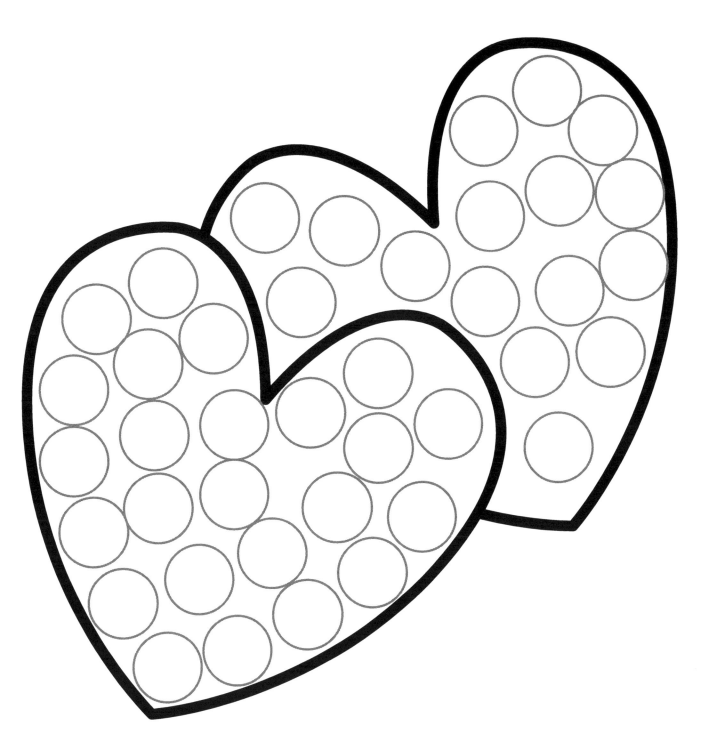

JESUS COMMANDED US TO LOVE ONE ANOTHER

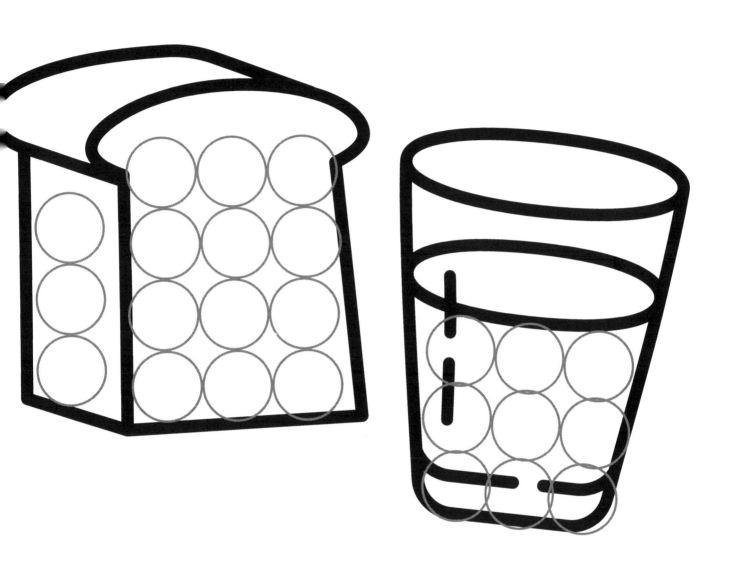

THE SACRAMENT HELPS
ME THINK OF JESUS

JESUS TEACHES HE IS THE VINE & WE ARE THE BRANCH-HE WANTS US TO STAY CLOSE TO HIM

JESUS SUFFERED BECAUSE HE LOVES ME

WE CAN PRAY TO HEAVENLY
FATHER WHEN WE NEED HELP

BECAUSE OF JESUS, WE WILL ALL BE ABLE TO BE RESURRECTED SOME DAY

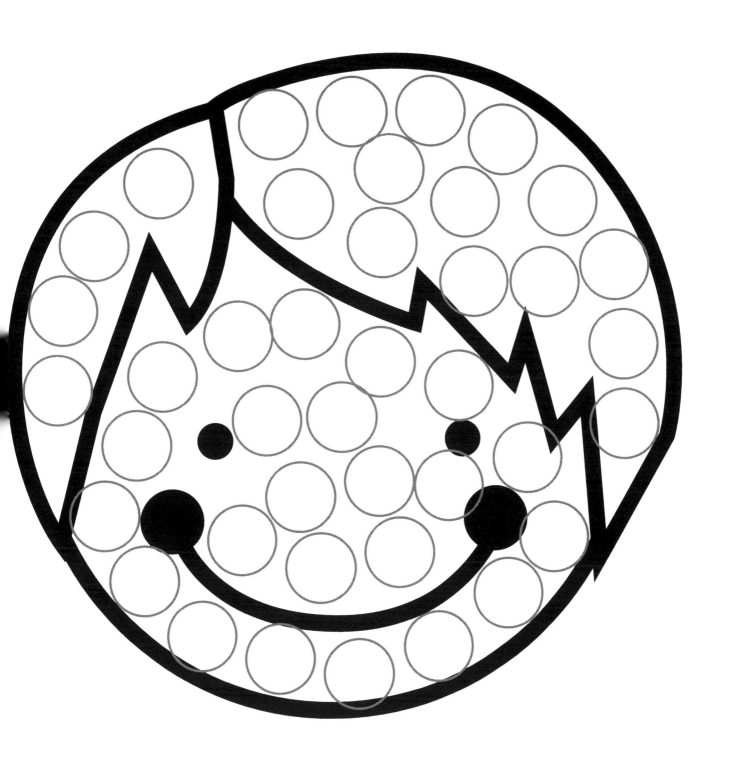

WE CAN BE FORGIVEN WHEN WE MAKE A MISTAKE

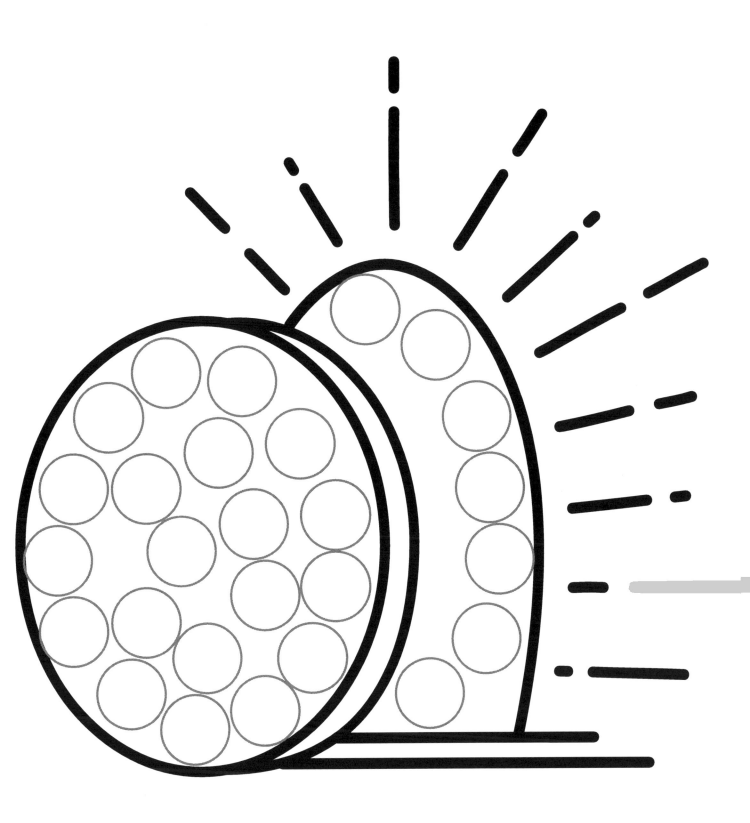

JESUS ROSE FROM THE TOMB

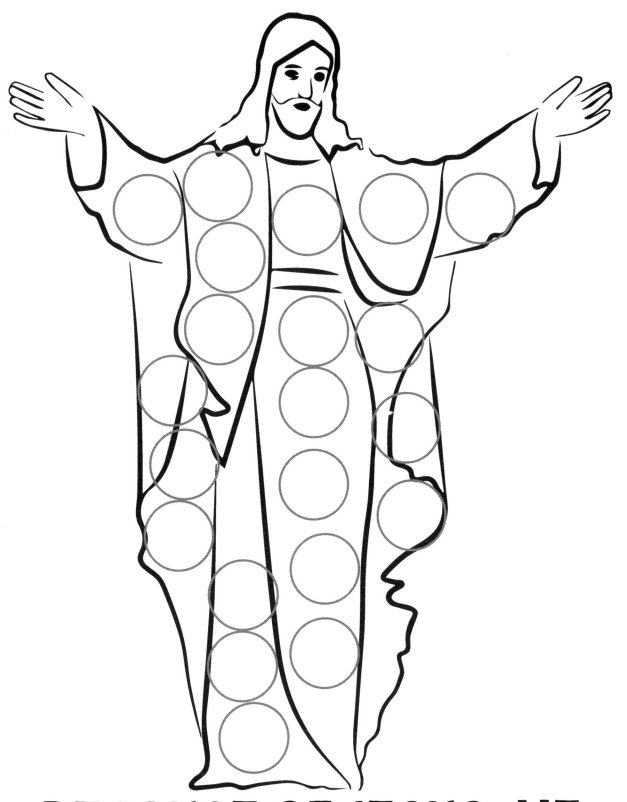

BECAUSE OF JESUS, WE WILL ALL LIVE AGAIN

IF YOU ENJOYED THIS BOOK, MAKE SURE TO LEAVE A REVIEW.

CHECK OUT OUR OTHER BOOKS!

FOLLOW US ONLINE!

@LATTER.DAY.DESIGNS

LATTER-DAY DESIGNS

Made in the USA
Columbia, SC
05 November 2024

45748964R00065